An American Bird Conservancy Compact Guide

Paul Lehman
Ornithological Editor

The American Bird Conservancy (ABC) is a U.S.-based, not-for-profit organization formed to unify bird conservation efforts across the Americas and dedicated to the conservation of birds throughout the Western Hemisphere. ABC practices conservation through partnership, bringing together the partners whose expertise and resources are best suited to each task.

The ABC Policy Council has a membership of more than 70 organizations sharing a common interest in the conservation of birds. Composed of ornithologists, policy specialists, educators, and general bird enthusiasts, the Council is a professional forum for exchanging information and discussing critical and emerging bird conservation issues. The Council provides policy and scientific advice to conservationists, stimulates a network of support for conservation policies through national, state, and local groups, and directly accomplishes conservation through ABC.

ABC is a working member of Partners in Flight (PIF), an Americas-wide coalition of more than 150 organizations and government agencies dedicated to bird conservation. Initially begun to find ways to reverse the decline in neotropical migratory bird species, PIF has broadened its scope to include all non-game birds in the Americas. PIF links birders, hunters, government, industry, landowners, and other citizens in a unified effort to conserve bird populations and habitats.

Many North American "birds" found in this guide spend more than half their lives in Latin America and the Caribbean. The needs for bird conservation in this region are at least as great as in the U.S. Through PIF, ABC is building U.S. support for capable, but often underfunded, conservation partners throughout the Americas.

PIF's bird conservation strategy, called the Flight Plan, can be obtained from ABC, the National Fish and Wildlife Foundation, or the U.S. Fish and Wildlife Service. PIF's National Coordinator serves on ABC's staff, and ABC helps implement the Flight Plan through its Important Bird Areas (IBA) initiative. ABC members receive Bird Conservation, the magazine about PIF and American bird conservation.

yellow-shafted flicker

ALL THE
SONG
BIRDS
EASTERN TRAILSIDE

BY JACK L. GRIGGS

HarperPerennial
A Division of HarperCollins*Publishers*

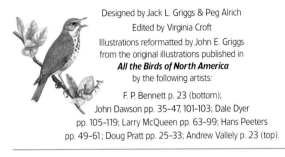

Designed by Jack L. Griggs & Peg Alrich

Edited by Virginia Croft

Illustrations reformatted by John E. Griggs
from the original illustrations published in
All the Birds of North America
by the following artists:

F. P. Bennett p. 23 (bottom);
John Dawson pp. 35-47, 101-103; Dale Dyer
pp. 105-119; Larry McQueen pp. 63-99; Hans Peeters
pp. 49-61; Doug Pratt pp. 25-33; Andrew Vallely p. 23 (top).

HarperCollins books may be purchased for educational, business, or sales
promotional use. For information, please write: Special Markets Department,
HarperCollins Publishers Inc., 10 East 53rd Street, New York, NY 10022.

FIRST EDITION

Library of Congress Cataloging-in-Publication Data is available on request.

ISBN 0-06-273694-9

00 01 02 03 04 PE 5 4 3 2 1

CONTENTS

EASTERN WOODLAND HABITATS
a foreword by Ron Rohrbaugh

EASTERN WOODLAND HABITATS

by *RON ROHRBAUGH*

NORTHERN HARDWOOD
(deciduous and mixed deciduous/coniferous)

white ash
quaking aspen
bigtooth aspen
American beech
yellow birch
black cherry
eastern hemlock
red maple
sugar maple
northern red oak
eastern white pine

CENTRAL BROAD-LEAVED
(deciduous and mixed deciduous/coniferous)

white ash
American basswood
yellow birch
flowering dogwood
eastern hemlock
several hickories
red maple
sugar maple
several oaks
eastern white pine
sweet gum

Of the six commonly recognized forest ecoregions in eastern North America, four occupy nearly all of the land area in the eastern US. Each contains numerous forest types based on regional and local conditions. Some of the common trees of each ecoregion are included in the sidebars on this and the facing page.

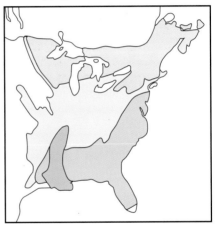

Modified from J. W. Duffield
Introduction to Forest Science (Wiley and Sons, 1990)

NORTHERN HARDWOOD FOREST

CENTRAL BROAD-LEAVED FOREST

SOUTHERN OAK-PINE FOREST

BOTTOMLAND HARDWOOD FOREST

SOUTHERN OAK-PINE
(deciduous and
coniferous)

eastern red cedar
flowering dogwood
several hickories
red maple
several oaks
loblolly pine
longleaf pine
shortleaf pine
slash pine

**BOTTOMLAND
HARDWOOD**
(mostly deciduous)

green ash
river birch
Atlantic white cedar
eastern cottonwood
bald cypress
box elder
honey locust
red maple
silver maple
several oaks
pecan
pond pine
sugarberry
sycamore
water tupelo

Birds are integral components of forest ecosystems. They use forests for food, cover, and nest sites and, in return, eat insects and disperse seeds. Seed caching by blue jays, for example, is an important mechanism for forest regeneration.

Each woodland bird has its own nesting habitat requirements. Some birds (specialists) have very specific needs met by a single forest type. Others (generalists) range through various types of woodlands. The following sections describe key characteristics influencing the distribution and abundance of birds in eastern forests. They will help anyone recognize and use the surrounding forest to predict the birds likely to be seen along a trail.

First, let's define a forest as any habitat composed mainly of woody vegetation (shrubs and trees). This includes clear-cuts and old fields just beginning to regenerate, forested wetlands, woodlots of all sizes and ages, and of course, the stereotypical expanse of mature trees.

Forest type, in general, is determined by the species of plants, mainly trees and shrubs, that dominate the landscape, such as "beech-maple" or "oak-hickory." Differences in forest type and climate among ecoregions account for the general distributions of birds in eastern North America. These ecoregions

7

can be used to define the ranges of some species. However, most species have ranges that overlap ecoregions.

Forest type within each ecoregion changes at both regional and local scales. At the regional scale, forest type is determined by differences in such variables as climate, soils, and topography. At the local scale, forest type is determined by such conditions as water level, elevation, and aspect (compass direction that a slope faces).

The presence, abundance, and movement of water are responsible for producing riparian forests and forested wetlands. Riparian forests are those that occur along moving water, such as rivers and creeks. From the air, a riparian forest looks like a ribbon of trees following the meandering path of the flowing water. Depending partly on the size of the water channel, the forest can extend inland from ten to more than a thousand feet.

Riparian forests are created by differences in soil type and moisture content as a result of flooding. These conditions favor trees such as green ash, sycamore, river birch, and silver maple. The cover and abundance of food a riparian forest provides — fruits, nuts, and especially flying insects — attract a diverse community of birds and other wildlife.

Trails commonly wind through riparian forests, and in summer, hikers may see rough-winged swallows zipping over the water or brilliant yellow warblers in the shrubs and trees. Other warblers can be found from ground to canopy. Flycatchers are often numerous along the edges of streams where bugs abound. Yellow-billed cuckoos are more often heard than seen. Listen for their distinctive *kakakaka-ka-ka-kow-kow-kowp-kowp-kowp* guttural call, starting fast and slowing at the end.

A forested wetland is another forest type created by the presence of water — in this case, standing water associated with poorly drained soils. Forested wetlands can range from dense shrubby habitats to mature forests including many standing dead trees.

BALD CYPRESS

In the southeastern US, forested wetlands often include bald cypress, southern magnolia, swamp chestnut oak, and swamp tupelo. The birds attracted include many of those found in riparian woodlands. Also look for the spectacular prothonotary warbler near the water and in overhanging vegetation. Great crested flycatchers often inhabit the canopy, and pileated woodpeckers put on a spectacular show with their flaming red crests and raucous calls.

In the Northeast, typical wetland trees include eastern hemlock, black gum, yellow birch, pin

9

oak, and pussy willow. Several species of birds are particularly fond of stands of eastern hemlock in forested wetlands: the Acadian flycatcher, blue-headed vireo, black-throated green warbler, and blackburnian warbler.

EASTERN HEMLOCK

Elevation and aspect differences can have significant effects on plant and bird communities. Increased elevation typically results in cooler temperatures and more precipitation. In parts of the Appalachians, there is a decrease of about three degrees Fahrenheit for every 1,000 feet gained in elevation. As a result, the prominent forest types on peaks above 4,500 feet in the Great Smoky Mountains (part of the Appalachians) of Tennessee and North Carolina are spruce-fir and northern hardwoods. At lower elevations, these same mountains are occupied by oak-hickory forests more typical of the Southeast. On south- and west-facing slopes with greater amounts of solar radiation, elevational effects are tempered.

RED SPRUCE

High-elevation forests of the Southeast often contain birds that are more commonly found in the northern US. These include the red-breasted nuthatch, brown creeper, dark-eyed junco, and common raven.

The peaks of the Appalachians range in height from the 6,684-foot-tall Mount Mitchell (North Carolina) to unnamed foothills less than 1,000 feet high. On the slopes of smaller peaks, the effects of aspect may be more pronounced than those of elevation. For example, in northern Pennsylvania and southern New York, where the Central Broad-leaved ecoregion gives way to the Northern Hardwood, one can often find American beech, sugar maple, yellow birch, and eastern hemlock growing on cool, moist north- and east-facing slopes, while the drier, warmer south- and west-facing slopes are occupied by oaks and hickories. As a result, there can be a difference in the bird community from one side of the mountain to the other.

SHAGBARK HICKORY

Forest age and structure are primary characteristics determining the composition of a bird community. As a forest ages, it goes through a process known as ecological succession. Plants and animals associated with one successional stage are replaced in succeeding stages with those better adapted for the new conditions.

Imagine walking through a 50-acre hayfield that was abandoned 15 years ago. "Ouch! I just got a thorn in my thigh. There must be some way out of these briars. It looks like we might be able to crawl through that opening over there." Does this sound like a familiar experience? If so, you must have visited what is called an "old field."

11

An old field is essentially the very beginning of a new forest. It is the first successional stage not dominated by herbaceous plants, such as grasses and forbs. At this stage, the new "forest" has no vertical layering. It is composed of woody shrubs and young trees that are mostly the same height.

Depending on where you are in eastern North America, there is a predictable community of plants and birds found in an old field. The plants tend to be low-growing shrubs and trees that tolerate full sun. These include blackberries, raspberries, hawthorns, honey-suckles, multiflora rose, black locust, eastern red cedar, and many others.

HAWTHORN

Birds nesting and foraging in old fields include brown thrashers, chats, eastern towhees, blue grosbeaks, field sparrows, and song sparrows. Owls and hawks often hunt in old fields.

Now imagine it's 20 years later. The same "field" now looks, smells, and sounds more like a forest. The site has already progressed through an early-successional forest stage dominated by sapling-sized trees of roughly uniform age and size. A few species of birds, such as chestnut-sided warblers and golden-winged warblers, may have come and gone because of the changing habitat.

The now-35-year-old midsuccessional forest contains small and medium-sized trees that you can easily wrap your arms around, and some you can get your hands around. These trees create an overhead canopy. An understory of shrubs and young trees will probably be developing below the canopy.

RHODODENDRON

Some of the plants in the understory are tolerant of shade and will always stay there. These may include mountain laurel, rhododendron, juneberry, witch hazel, and viburnums. Young, continually growing trees, the offspring of those forming the canopy, also dot the understory.

The two vertical layers, understory and canopy, contain a diverse selection of foods and nest sites that attract a wide variety of birds. Among the most beautiful canopy dwellers in a midsuccessional forest are the American redstart and the Baltimore oriole. Wood thrushes, ovenbirds, and hooded warbers are prominent understory species.

Forty years later the oldest trees have been standing for 75 years, and important changes have occurred. Some trees have grown quite large (many are too big to fully wrap your arms around), some have died, some have fallen, and vertical layering has increased.

13

Late-successional forests usually supply the greatest amount of vertical layering. Working from the ground up, it's possible to have several layers, including an understory of shrubs, an intermediate (or subdominant) canopy of small trees, a codominant canopy of medium-sized trees, and a primary canopy (overstory) of larger trees.

The habitat diversification associated with this vertical layering supports a tremendous diversity of birds. For example, veeries and hermit thrushes thrive in the understory; red-eyed vireos and rose-breasted grosbeaks forage above them in the intermediate canopy; while scarlet tanagers and black-throated green warblers glean insects from the codominant and primary canopies.

Dead and dying trees, known as snags, provide a smorgasbord of food for insectivorous birds. Snags and hollow trees also provide nesting and roosting cavities for many birds, the largest cavities being used by screech-owls and barred owls.

Even fallen trees continue to be useful to birds, providing cover and foraging sites for those that dwell close to the ground. They also create openings or gaps in the forest canopy, thus allowing sunlight to penetrate to the forest floor. These tiny gaps support herbaceous and sun-loving plants that add habitat diversity to the forest ecosystem.

Forest edge occurs where trees meet fields, stream, roads, or housing developments, for instance. Edges can be great places to find birds, and hiking trails often follow the contour of an edge. During summer and winter, expect to see an abundance and diversity of common birds along edges. During spring and fall migration, edges can be spectacular places to find migrating warblers, vireos, and sparrows. Sometimes edges follow the border of migration barriers, such as bays and large lakes. These are favored places for birds to rest and refuel while making long migratory journeys.

Although edges provide diversity, food, and opportunity for many birds, they do not provide safety for nesting. Edges provide easy access for predators, such as raccoons, feral cats, chipmunks, crows, and jays, in search of nests for an easy meal.

Brown-headed cowbirds have taken advantage of the creation of habitat edges to become a threat to some eastern songbirds. A midwestern grassland species, cowbirds invaded the East as forests were cleared for agriculture. They do not build nests or raise their own young but rather lay eggs in a host bird's nest. The cowbird nestling generally hatches first, outcompetes the host's nestlings for food, and is often the only nestling to survive and fledge.

Loss and fragmentation of eastern forests has dramatically affected bird communities. Until the late 18th century, the extensive and contiguous eastern forest remained largely intact. By the 1850s, however, an estimated 114 million acres had been converted to agriculture, and much of the remaining forestland had been cut over at least once.

By the 1920s, the Carolina parakeet was extinct and Bachman's warbler and the ivory-billed woodpecker were doomed, in part because of deforestation. Then the clearing of forests in the East slowed, and farms began to be abandoned. The reversion of farmland back to forest has increased the amount of forestland in the conterminous US by over 20 percent. But much of the eastern forest is now in fragments (patches) separated by nonforest habitats.

A patch's size and shape will cause some birds to be absent from habitats that otherwise appear to be suitable. For example, a mature but small 15-acre woodlot in the Central Broad-leaved ecoregion is likely to support great-crested flycatchers, Baltimore orioles, and indigo buntings. However, it is unlikely to support area-sensitive species, such as black-and-white warblers, ovenbirds, or veeries.

Long, narrow patches provide less safe interior habitat than round or square patches.

Today's forests are being lost and degraded primarily through residential, commercial, and industrial development, along with road construction. Most bird species of eastern forests are still abundant, but the ultimate effects of contemporary forest loss and degradation on birds may be greater than the large-scale clearing of the past century, because forest loss owing to development is permanent.

During the 1980s, biologists and birders began to notice long-term population declines among neotropical migratory birds (species that nest in temperate regions of North America and migrate to Central and South America and the Caribbean to spend the winter). Among the declining species were birds that depend on extensive mature forests, such as the wood thrush and the cerulean warbler.

Biologists have learned much about the threats that forest birds face. It's now time to begin applying what we've learned about bird conservation and forest management to reverse existing population declines and ensure that common species remain common, so that we can always enjoy the multicolored flash of a painted bunting zipping across a trail or the ethereal song of a veery at dusk.

HOW TO LOOK AT A BIRD

The way birds feed and their adaptations for feeding are the most important points to recognize in identifying and understanding a bird. For the beginner, the color and pattern of an unknown bird can be so striking that important points of shape and behavior go unnoticed. But feeding adaptations, especially bill shape, best reveal a bird's role in nature — its truest identity.

Owls, hawks, doves, woodpeckers, and many other birds are easily recognized by shape and behavior. Songbirds are more confusing. If you don't immediately recognize a songbird as a sparrow, a wren, or a warbler, for example, try to see its bill shape. Is it a seed-crusher or a bug-eater? Seed-crushers have strong, conical bills for cracking seeds. The shape of a bug-eater's bill varies with the way it catches bugs.

conical bill

Most bug-eaters have slender, straight bills used to probe in trees, brush, ground litter, and rock crevices. A few have curved bills for specialized probing. And some, the flycatcher group, have broad-based, flat bills. Flycatchers catch bugs in midair, and their broad bills improve their chances of success.

straight bill

curved bill

flycatching bill

If bill shape can't be seen, a bird's feeding behavior is often just as revealing. Sparrows don't flit among the branches of a tree searching for bugs, and warblers won't be seen on the ground picking at seeds.

Knowing its bill shape or feeding behavior reduces the possible identities of an unknown songbird. Plumage marks can then be used to identify all the trailside songbirds.

Most names used to describe parts of a bird are predictable — back, crown, throat, etc. Three names that might not be immediately understood are rump, undertail coverts, and wing bars. The rump is at the base of the tail, topside; undertail coverts cover the base of the tail, bottomside. Wing bars are formed by the contrasting tips (often white) of the feathers that help cover the wing when it is folded.

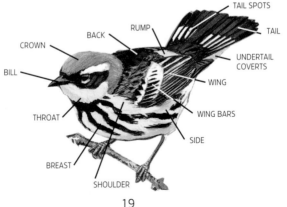

HOW TO READ THE MAPS

Range maps provide a simplified picture of a species' distribution. They indicate the birds that can be expected in any local region. Birds are not evenly distributed over their ranges. They require suitable habitat (no seeds, no sparrows) and are typically scarcest at their range limits. Some birds are numerous but not commonly seen because they are secretive.

Weather and food availability affect bird distribution in winter. Some birds regularly retreat to warmer southern weather or to the narrow coastal band where the Gulf and Atlantic moderate the worst of the winter. Other birds are adapted to successfully forage — a few even nest and raise their young — in freezing Arctic winds and drifting snow.

MAP KEY

SUMMER OR
NESTING

WINTER

ALL YEAR

MIGRATION
(spring & fall)

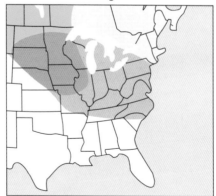

HOW THE BIRDS ARE ORGA- NIZED

Not all woodpeckers are called woodpeckers — flickers and sapsuckers, for instance, are also woodpeckers. In the list below, birds with names different from their common group name are listed in parentheses following the group name.

21

CHIMNEY SWIFT

ROUGH-WINGED SWALLOW

TREE SWALLOW

RUBY-THROATED HUMMINGBIRD

The small aerialists that can be seen from woodland trails are summer visitors over most of North America. Swifts and swallows collect insects in flight and prefer open areas for feeding. For flocks of **chimney swifts,** that includes the open skies over woodlands. They won't be seen perching on a limb or wire; they must be identified in flight. Their rapid, erratic flight style is distinctive, and their shallow, stiff wing beats create a twinkling effect that, once noted, is easily recognized.

Tree swallows are numerous and venture into woodland edges for nesting cavities. The glossy blue-green back and rump of the adult **tree swallow** are distinctive. The dingy brown breast is the key mark for **rough-winged swallows.** Young tree swallows are white below, but some can show a dusky breast band. Rough-winged swallows often feed over woodland streams.

Hummingbirds aren't much concerned with the type of woodland they inhabit. They are preoccupied with flowers, which provide them with nectar. Tiny insects are their source of protein. The **ruby-throated hummingbird** is the only eastern hummer. The throat of the male usually appears black. Only when light reflects at a favorable angle can the dazzling ruby red be seen. From the back, males can be identified by their deeply notched tails.

Chimney Swift

Rough-winged
Swallow

young

Tree Swallow

Ruby-throated
Hummingbird

♀   ♂

PILEATED WOODPECKER

PILEATED WOODPECKER

Because of their size, pileated woodpeckers need large trees for nesting and roosting. They are usually seen in old forests, but look for them also in younger woods with scattered large dead trees. They feed on ants and beetle larvae in live and decaying wood. Nuts and berries are also taken seasonally.

By the 1900s, pileateds were rare in the East because of the destruction of the original forest. They have gradually increased since then with forest regrowth. The disastrous Dutch elm disease has aided pileateds by providing them with dead trees for nesting and shelter.

Excavating a nest cavity typically takes several weeks and is usually done in a dead tree. Pileateds sometimes roost in nest cavities but typically use a hollow tree, drilling several holes for entrance and escape from predators. Numerous other animals, including mammals, birds, reptiles, and insects, depend on the excavating abilities of the pileated woodpecker for their own shelter and nests.

A crow-sized bird, the **pileated woodpecker** is quite distinctive and not likely to be confused with crows or other woodpeckers. Note the red moustache mark on the male. A loud drumming or a *wuk-wuk-wuk-wuk* call is often heard before the bird is seen.

Pileated
Woodpecker

♀

♂

WOOD-PECKERS

DOWNY WOODPECKER

HAIRY WOODPECKER

The most common woodpecker in eastern woodlands is the downy. It is also the smallest, just 7 inches long. The hairy woodpecker has virtually the identical plumage pattern but is 2 inches larger. Both species are seen throughout eastern forests, feeding primarily on insects and larvae.

Unless the two species are seen side by side, their size difference can be hard to recognize. The best mark separating them is bill length. The **hairy woodpecker** has a much larger bill — nearly as long as its head. The **downy woodpecker's** bill extends only about half its head length. The hairy also gives a noticeably sharper *peek!* call than the downy.

Males of both species have a bright red patch on the back of their crowns that is lacking in females. Young birds (both sexes) also show a patch of red on their heads, but the color is more diffuse and is located on the center or forepart of the crown rather than on the rear.

There is a very small plumage difference that can be noted on birds at close range. The white outer tail feathers on the hairy woodpecker are unmarked, while those on the downy woodpecker have two or more black bars.

young

hairy

Downy
Woodpecker

♀

♂

♀

Hairy
Woodpecker

♂

WOOD-PECKERS

RED-HEADED WOODPECKER

RED-BELLIED WOODPECKER

Red-headed woodpeckers were once numerous. The introduction of the starling from Europe a century ago caused the red-headed's numbers to greatly diminish, especially in the Northeast. Starlings compete successfully with the red-headed woodpecker for nest holes.

Open woodlands (deciduous, pine, or mixed) are favorite haunts of both red-headed and red-bellied woodpeckers. The red-headed's range extends on to prairies, where it sometimes makes cavities in utility poles. The red-bellied's habitat includes swamps and more densely forested lands. Neither bird is shy; they are often seen in suburban shade trees.

Red-bellied woodpeckers are much more numerous than red-headed woodpeckers. Both are versatile feeders, and they both fly with the deep, undulating flight characteristic of woodpeckers. They can be seen on the ground as well as in trees and have a varied diet, including insects, nuts, seeds, fruit, and berries. Flying insects are frequently taken, especially by the red-headed.

The bright colors and sharp patterns of the two woodpeckers are distinctive. Note that the female **red-bellied woodpecker** lacks the red crown of the male. The red-bellied's name comes from the faint red wash on the belly, which is often not seen at all.

Young **red-headed woodpeckers** have a brown head and dark bars on their white wing patches. They acquire the impressive red-headed adult plumage over their first winter.

young

Red-headed
Woodpecker

Red-bellied
Woodpecker

♂

♀

FLICKER & SAPSUCKER

YELLOW-SHAFTED FLICKER

YELLOW-BELLIED SAPSUCKER

The rare and endangered red-cockaded woodpecker lives in small colonies in open stands of mature pines in the South.

It is black and white and has a "ladder-back" like the red-bellied woodpecker (p. 28). The face is largely white.

Flickers and sapsuckers are woodpeckers, and they both prefer open woodlands or forest edges. Flickers are often seen foraging for ants on the ground under trees. Sapsuckers drill rings of sap wells in trees and return to feed on the sap and insects attracted to it. The trees — hundreds of varieties are used — are undamaged, and the wells feed many animals.

The yellow-shafted flicker is the form of northern flicker seen in the East, where it is numerous. (A tail feather with the yellow shaft is shown on the title page of this book). The plumage is unmistakable, but the birds are shy and often fly off at a distance. They are often not recognized as a woodpecker by those unfamiliar with them because they typically take off from the ground.

The best marks for the **yellow-shafted flicker** are the white rump patch and the flash of yellow seen in the wings as it flies away. At close range, females can be seen to lack the black mustache mark of the male.

Female **yellow-bellied sapsuckers** lack the male's red throat. Young yellow-bellieds are brownish through their first winter, but have the distinctive white stripe on their wings seen in adults. Sapsuckers are shy, retiring, and less numerous than flickers.

Yellow-shafted Flicker

young

♂

♀

♂

Yellow-bellied
Sapsucker

NUTHATCHES & CREEPER

WHITE-BREASTED NUTHATCH

RED-BREASTED NUTHATCH

BROWN CREEPER

The brown-headed nuthatch inhabits southern and coastal pines. About the size of a red-breasted nuthatch, it has a brown cap with a white nape spot.

Nuthatches and the brown creeper cling to the sides of trees like woodpeckers, searching for insects and larvae hidden in a tree's bark. Nuthatches are the only tree-climbers so agile that they can creep down a tree. Presumably, they find morsels that upward-climbers miss.

The **white-breasted nuthatch** is numerous. It is most common in open deciduous woodlands but can be found on any large tree. Females are the same as males, except some are noticeably grayer on the crown. There is an inconspicuous wash of rusty red on the flanks.

Red-breasted nuthatches are smaller and less common than the white-breasted. They have rusty red underparts and a black eye stripe; females are duller than males. They prefer conifers, especially in summer. In winter, they are widely distributed. Like the white-breasted, they like tree trunks and large limbs but also take seeds from pine cones and insects from the tips of small branches.

The **brown creeper** is fairly numerous in mature forests but often overlooked because it is quiet and blends in well with the tree trunks it frequents. It spirals up a large trunk inconspicuously and is often first noticed when it flies from one tree trunk to the base of another.

White-breasted Nuthatch

♀

Red-breasted Nuthatch ♂

Brown Creeper

WAXWING AND SHRIKE

CEDAR WAXWING

LOGGERHEAD SHRIKE

Cedar waxwing numbers have increased in the last 20 years, while shrikes have decreased. The conversion of farms to woodlands and suburbs is partly responsible for both.

Woodlands and suburbs provide fruiting plants for waxwings while diminishing the open field habitat in which shrikes hunt.

Waxwings nest in open woodlands. During the summer, they feed heavily on insects and are often seen near water where insects abound. Over the rest of the year, they wander in flocks of up to a hundred birds or so, searching for sugar-rich fruits (cedar berries are a favorite) as they come into season. Flocks keep in close contact with pleasing high-pitched, lisping calls.

The small dots of red on the wings of the **cedar waxwing** suggest the wax once used for sealing documents and are the source of the bird's name. The crest, narrow black mask, and yellow tail tip are easy identifying marks. Their upright posture and fastidiously smooth plumage give waxwings a military bearing.

Loggerhead shrikes are patterned much like the lankier mockingbird, but note the black mask, big head, and compact body. Young loggerhead shrikes have fine dark barring on their breasts and backs until fall.

Shrikes hunt alone over open country and nest in shrubs and scattered trees. Like the waxwing, they feed heavily on flying insects in summer, and both birds have broad-based bills like those of flycatchers. When the insect population collapses in fall, shrikes depend on a diet of small animals, including songbirds.

34

Cedar Waxwing

young

Loggerhead Shrike

shrike

mockingbird
p. 46

FLYCATCHERS

OLIVE-SIDED
FLYCATCHER

EASTERN
KINGBIRD

GREAT CRESTED
FLYCATCHER

The posture of the eastern kingbird illustrated is typical of the female. Males tend to raise their crowns more prominently and sit more vertically, like the flycatchers above and below in the illustration.

lycatchers, including kingbirds, typically sit on an exposed perch and wait for an insect to pass by. It is their patient waiting that is often the first clue to their identity. Most songbirds busily search the forest for insects; flycatchers sit and search the sky.

After a foray for an insect, flycatchers often return to the same perch. The **olive-sided flycatcher** almost inevitably returns to the same dead snag. It is scarce in cool coniferous forests of the North and high Appalachians — often near water. Larger than the similar fly-catchers in the next illustration, it is also distin-guished by its vest-like gray sides.

Eastern kingbirds hunt from wires or promi-nent perches in woodland edges and open areas. They are numerous, noisy, and aggres-sive birds that are seldom overlooked. The white tail tip is the clinching mark.

Great crested flycatchers are as noisy and ag-gressive as kingbirds but often much less visi-ble. They hide in the canopy of shade trees or trees in open woods and forest edges. Listen for their piercing *wheeep!* call. The rusty red flash in the wings and tail are good marks when a **great crested flycatcher** emerges from foliage to catch a passing bug (compare with the yellow-billed cuckoo on p. 41).

Olive-sided
Flycatcher

Eastern
Kingbird

Great Crested Flycatcher

EASTERN PHOEBE

EASTERN WOOD-PEWEE

EMPIDONAX FLYCATCHERS

Phoebes give a *fee-bee, fee-bay* song, the last syllable in each pair alternately rising and falling. The eastern wood-pewee's song is a plaintive *pee-a-wee*.

The familiar phoebes that nest on building ledges and bridges are also found in woodlands, where they use the rocky outcrops and other natural ledges that were their original nest sites — especially those near water. Because they feed on berries and fruits as well as flying insects, they can remain much farther north in winter than birds that are strictly flycatchers.

Pewees are numerous and widespread in most eastern woodlands. They often flycatch at edges and clearings or within a closed canopy if it is relatively free of underbrush. Unlike most flycatchers, pewees seem to prefer drier sites away from water.

There are five different empidonax species in the East, and they all look much alike. Some are a little yellower below and greener above than others, but variation can be due more to plumage wear than species differences. Separating species can confound experts.

Empids, pewees, and phoebes are often confused but can be reliably separated with a good look. Most **empids** have wing bars and eye-rings; **pewees** have wing bars but no eye-rings; **phoebes** have neither, although young birds have buff wing bars. A good mark for the phoebe is its downward tail-pumping habit.

38

Eastern Phoebe

Eastern Wood-Pewee

Empidonax Flycatchers

typical fresh
fall plumage

typical worn
summer plumage

THRASHER & CUCKOO

BROWN THRASHER

YELLOW-BILLED CUCKOO

Black-billed cuckoos are scarce northern relatives of the yellow-billed. Where ranges overlap, black-billeds occupy higher and often shrubbier areas.

Tail spots are much smaller in the black-billed, and it lacks reddish wings or a yellow bill spot. Its call is a monotonous *cu-cu-cu-cu.*

hrashers typically feed on the ground, tossing ground clutter aside with their curved bills to uncover bugs. They are shy birds that, when discovered in the open, quickly return to brushy cover. They are fairly numerous in forested and open landscapes where brush or shrubbery is present.

The reddish upperparts and streaked underparts of the **brown thrasher** are similar to the markings of the wood thrush (p. 56). However, thrashers are more elongated, have a curved bill, and streaks — not round spots — below.

Cuckoos are furtive birds that inhabit mature woods, as well as second-growth (such as overgrown pastures) and waterside willow thickets. They do much of their foraging in trees and vegetation and are especially fond of caterpillars.

Cuckoos are fairly numerous, but much less so than brown thrashers. The white spots on the undertail of the **yellow-billed cuckoo** are good marks when the bird is not concealed in vegetation. Often the best view is when one flies swiftly from one concealing tree to another. In flight, note the long tail and rusty red color in the wings. Listen for their gradually slowing, guttural call, *kakakaka-kow-kow-kow—kowp—kowp—kowp.*

40

Brown Thrasher

Yellow-billed Cuckoo

young

WINTER WREN

HOUSE WREN

CAROLINA WREN

Carolina wren populations gradually extend northward beyond the dashed line on the map following mild winters, only to crash after a severe winter.

Wrens are small, energetic bug-eaters usually seen in shrubs and dense underbrush on or near the ground. Although shy, they are loquacious and can often be located by the noisy scolding they give when approached too closely.

Winter wrens are scarce and, as the name implies, are seen in winter (and fall) over most of the US. In summer, they retreat to the cool, dense undergrowth of northern and high Appalachian conifers. They are the smallest of the wrens, but overall size can be difficult to judge in the field. It is the very stubby, erect tail that is the best mark for the **winter wren.** Also note the pronounced black-and-white barring on the sides.

Mousy brown **house wrens** are numerous in woodlots and forest edges, as well as in residential areas. Although short, the barred tail is noticeably longer than that of the winter wren. There is some indistinct barring on the sides.

Carolina wrens are numerous residents likely to be encountered in any patch of eastern woods, especially in wet or moist areas. They are also familiar birds around suburban residences. The white eye stripe, reddish back and tail, and cinnamon underparts are all easy marks for the **Carolina wren.**

42

Winter Wren

House Wren

Carolina Wren

AMERICAN CROW

COMMON RAVEN

Crows and their larger relatives, ravens, are the most intelligent North American birds. This is an opinion rooted in Native American folklore and confirmed by present-day ornithologists. Crows and ravens are not restricted to a specific diet but will take whatever is available. Their adaptability has permitted them to flourish. Crows are everywhere except deserts, mountain forests, and the Arctic. Ravens are increasing in the Appalachians and New England but are scarce in much of the East.

Separating the larger **common raven** from the **American crow** is usually just a matter of estimating size and noting tail shape. The raven's wedge-shaped tail is usually easy to distinguish from the crow's blunt tail. Also note the heavier bill and shaggy neck. Their call is a hoarse, low-pitched *c-r-ock*. Ravens are much more adept aerialists than crows.

Ornithologists recognize two crow species in the East, the American crow and the fish crow. The fish crow is slightly the smaller and is associated with coasts and rivers, but can appear well inland, especially at landfills. It is virtually indistinguishable from American crows in the field except for its distinct, nasal *eh-eh* call — not the familiar *cah* of the American crow.

American Crow

Common Raven

MOCKINGBIRD AND BLUE JAY

MOCKINGBIRD

BLUE JAY

The endangered Florida scrub-jay is found in central Florida, primarily in scrub oak. It lacks the blue jay's crest and is a mixture of blues and grays

The gray jay, a crest-less sooty-gray bird, is numerous in the conifers of Canada and portions of Michigan, Minnesota, and northern New England.

The mockingbird and blue jay are familiar suburban birds throughout the East. They originally lived in forested habitat and still do. Mockingbirds like parklands (brushy areas with scattered trees) and forest edge, where they can feed on the ground. They also pick fruit from bushes and trees. The only bird that much resembles a **mockingbird** is the loggerhead shrike (p. 34).

Blue jays, with their distinctive crests, prefer deciduous and mixed forests, especially beech and oak woods, which provide them with two of their favorite nuts. They collect and store the nuts, carrying one in a throat pouch and another in the bill. Nuts aren't their only food; a blue jay is omnivorous. So is the mockingbird.

Although they come from two different families (jays are in the same family as crows and magpies; DNA research shows mockingbirds are most closely related to starlings), blue jays and mockingbirds share other traits besides their fondness for suburbia and a varied diet. Both are conspicuous, noisy, aggressive, territorial birds, and both are good mimics.

The mocker, of course, is named for its celebrated mimicry. Blue jays give a great imitation of the red-shouldered hawk's *kee-yah* call, as well as the calls of other birds.

Mockingbird

young

Blue Jay

BLACK BIRDS

BROWN-HEADED COWBIRD

RUSTY BLACKBIRD

COMMON GRACKLE

Cowbird hosts seldom raise their own chicks successfully. Some eastern songbirds, including several warblers, are seriously threatened by cowbird parasitism.

Cowbirds and grackles live and feed in open fields but use trees at the edges of woodlands or in fragmented woods for nesting and roosting. Cowbirds are invaders from the West that lay their eggs in other birds' nests and abandon them to the care of the unwitting hosts. They and grackles have multiplied until they have become serious pests.

Rusty blackbirds often join mixed flocks of blackbirds, cowbirds, and grackles in winter, but they are seldom seen in fields. They are woodland birds fond of bogs and swamps, where they often wade in shallow water to feed.

The **brown-headed cowbird** is the smallest of the black birds, and the male has a brown head. Females are a mousy gray-brown, slightly paler below.

In winter, when **rusty blackbirds** are seen in most of the US, their feathers are rusty tipped. The amount and pattern of rusty brown vary with age and sex, with some individuals as brown as illustrated. By summer, the rusty tips wear away. Males are jet black with a slight green sheen. Females are slate gray.

Common grackles are lanky, long-tailed birds. Males are larger and have the most sheen. The sheen can be an overall purplish blue, or in many areas the body can be glossy bronze.

molting
fall young

♀

♂

**Brown-headed
Cowbird**

winter

summer

Rusty Blackbird

Common Grackle

STARLING

RED-WINGED BLACKBIRD

There are now an estimated 200 million descendants of the approximately 100 starlings first imported from Europe and released in New York City's Central Park in the early 1890s.

Flocks of starlings are abundant in urban parks, suburban lawns, and farm fields, where they walk in search of seeds, grains, and a variety of animal life. Some live in relatively wild areas and use woodlands to provide them with tree cavities in which to nest. Nest cavities are a limited resource, and the success of the starling comes at the expense of bluebirds and other native cavity nesters.

In all its varied plumages, the **starling's** very short tail and long, sharply pointed bill give it a distinctive look. Winter birds are heavily spotted with white on the feather tips, which wear away to reveal a glossy black plumage by spring.

Although primarily a bird of marshes and fields, the abundant red-winged blackbird also lives in open woodlands, especially near water. Like starlings, they feed from the ground on a variety of items. Many also gather insects and seeds from marsh vegetation.

The brilliant shoulder patch of the male **red-winged blackbird** is often hidden when the bird is perched, and only the buff border is revealed. Female red-wings are smaller than males and suggest a large sparrow with a hint of red on the face and shoulder. The sexes often flock separately.

young

Starling

spring

fall

Red-winged Blackbird

young

ORCHARD ORIOLE

BALTIMORE ORIOLE

Orchard and Baltimore orioles like to nest and feed in scattered trees and forest edges, especially near water. Both readily accept suburban shade trees as well. When nesting, they live on insects and spiders. Fruit is added to their diet the rest of the year.

Adult male orioles are unmistakable, but females and young birds can be confusing. Female **orchard orioles** are olive green above and yellow to yellow-green below, with two white wing bars. They lack the orange tones of the female Baltimore oriole and are smaller.

Young orchard orioles in their first fall look very much like the female. The young males take two years to become adult, and the year-ling male has a black chin and throat that distinguish it from females and younger birds.

Female and young **Baltimore orioles** are particularly variable. Some females can show a lot of black on the head or throat (similar to a young male) and have warm orange tones below. Other females, particularly young birds, can be yellowish and plain, with only a tinge of orange. Yearling males show orange and black splotches. Female orioles are sometimes confused with female tanagers (p. 54), but eastern tanagers lack wing bars and have a "swollen" bill.

52

young ♂

Orchard Oriole

♀

♂

Baltimore Oriole

♀

♂

young ♂

TANAGERS

SCARLET TANAGER

SUMMER TANAGER

Tanagers are fairly numerous spring migrants and summer visitors in woodlands and shade trees. More would be seen if they weren't so often in the canopy of mature trees gathering insects. The scarlet tanager is widespread in mixed and deciduous forests. Its robin-like raspy, whistled phrases can be heard from the canopy of dense or open woodlands. The call is also hoarse, a two-noted *chip-burr.*

The brilliant body plumage of the male **scarlet tanager** lasts only through summer. By fall, males begin molting to a yellowish green body like the female's, but the wings and tail remain distinctively black. Patchy males can be seen before fall migration.

Summer tanagers like open woodlands (especially pine-oak) and woodland edges. Their song is clearer than the scarlet tanager's, and their call is a staccato *pit-i-tuck* of two to five notes. They take a variety of bugs but specialize in bees and wasps caught in flight or their grubs taken at the nest. They remove the stinger by wiping the dead insect against a branch.

Adult male **summer tanagers** are rosy red all year. Females aren't as green as female scarlet tanagers; note the larger bill and yellow edging on the wing feathers. Yearling males and some females show uneven reddish washes.

spring ♂

Scarlett Tanager

fall molting ♂

♀

♂

Summer Tanager

yearling ♂

♀

ROBIN

WOOD THRUSH

Wood thrushes are one of the songbirds most victimized by the brown-headed cowbird (p. 48). Their numbers have decreased steadily in many regions for the last 20 years.

R obins are members of the thrush family. They and wood thrushes are both birds of the forest floor. Robins like open, sunny clearings and edges in mature forests, where they search for earthworms and bugs, just as they do in lawns.

Female **robins** are distinctively duller above and paler orange below than males. Their young are spotted below, like typical thrushes. Robins seen in a forest are often shy, and their colors seem bright.

The wood thrush prefers the shadows and cover of tall trees with a closed canopy and substantial underbrush, especially damp areas, where they search leaf litter for various bugs. Like all thrushes, they are accomplished singers. Their rich, whistled, flute-like notes, *eee-o-lay,* are given in three- to five-note phrases that often end with a trill.

There are several spotted thrushes in the next illustration that resemble the wood thrush. All are birds of the forest floor or low bushes, and all look much alike, gray-brown to reddish brown above and pale below with breast spots.

The bold spots and the white — not buff — breast are good marks for the **wood thrush.** Also note the contrast of the rusty head and back with the browner rump and tail.

56

Wood Thrush

young

Robin

young

SWAINSON'S
THRUSH

VEERY

HERMIT THRUSH

Gray-cheeked and
Bicknell's thrushes
are less commonly
seen eastern thrush-
es. Both resemble
Swainson's but lack
an eye-ring and buff
on the face.

Swainson's thrush and the veery are woodland migrants over most of the East. In
their northern nesting territories, Swainson's
prefers coniferous forests, especially spruce;
veeries are most numerous in damp hardwood
forests with extensive understory. The hermit
thrush occupies a variety of woodlands. It is the
only spot-breasted thrush wintering in the US.

Back color, face pattern, and breast spotting
are important marks for thrushes. The **veery's**
back is an even tawny brown, and it has the
least conspicuous breast spotting. **Swainson's**
has a darker, but again, evenly colored back;
breast spots are more conspicuous. Also note
the buff eye-ring and facial markings.

Back color on **hermit thrushes** varies, but
eastern birds are brownish. Most important,
their tails are a contrasting rusty red and are
habitually pumped slowly.

Thrushes are often heard singing, sometimes
in migration. Swainson's gives an ascending
swirl of flute-like notes described as *whip-
poor-will-a-will-e-zee-zee-zee*. The veery is
named for its song, a descending series that
includes down-sliding *veer* or *vee-ur* notes.
The hermit thrush's song has been described
as *oh, holy-holy, ah, purity-purity, ehh, sweetly-
sweetly*, ascending but less so than Swainson's.

Swainson's Thrush

Veery

gray
western form

Hermit Thrush

eastern
form

CHAT

CATBIRD

**EASTERN
BLUEBIRD**

Chats are declining in
the East as second-
growth woodlands
increasingly reach
maturity. Some chats
have orange breasts
from a diet of honey-
suckle berries.

The chat and catbird are skulkers best known for their songs of jumbled whistles, squawks, and odd notes. Brush, shrubs, and vine tangles are their choice of habitat; bugs and berries, their favorite foods. They are also found in early second-growth woods, streamside thickets, and brushy forest edges. Catbirds are fairly numerous; chats, scarcer.

The **chat's** distinctive face pattern sets it apart from other birds with yellow breasts. The lores (areas between the white stripes) are black in the male, gray in the female. The **catbird** is gray with a contrasting black cap and tail. The rusty patch under the tail can be hard to see.

Bluebirds feed on fruit and ground insects. They don't probe for bugs in leaf litter as other ground feeders do, but take a low perch over open ground and scan the area below, fluttering down to inspect anything interesting. They nest in tree cavities and in the hundreds of thousands of nest boxes set out for them by volunteers. Bluebirds inhabit open woodlands and forest edges, as well as orchards and fields.

Family groups of **bluebirds** are often seen together in summer. Young birds are spotted below, like a thrush (p. 58), to which they are closely related. Young males have extensive blue in the wings and tail; females have less.

60

Chat

Catbird

young

♀

♂

Eastern Bluebird

VIREOS

RED-EYED VIREO

WARBLING VIREO

Philadelphia vireos are scarce migrants over most of the East in spring and fall. They nest in the deciduous forests of Canada and a few border states.

Their faces are similar to the warbling vireo's but more boldly marked. The best mark is a pale yellow breast. The warbling vireo shows yellow only on its sides.

The vireos in this illustration and the next are easily confused with each other and some of the warblers that follow. Vireos have thicker bills than warblers. Most are also more deliberate, even sluggish, feeders than the typical active warbler. Be sure to check the bill shape of any plain or yellowish warbler-like bird; it might be a vireo.

Red-eyed and warbling vireos have pale eyebrows and plain wings; those in the next illustration have spectacles and wing bars. The eyebrow and bordering stripes of the **red-eyed vireo** are pronounced. There is also a notable contrast between the gray cap and the yellow-green hind neck and back. The red eye usually looks dark. On the **warbling vireo,** the eyebrow and eye line are dull; spring birds have little green on their backs or yellow on their sides, but fall birds are often brighter.

The red-eyed vireo is one of the most abundant songbirds in eastern deciduous forests. Warbling vireos are more scattered, usually near water. However, both are birds of the treetops and often go unseen. They feed sluggishly on insects gleaned from foliage and are tireless singers. Red-eyed vireos sing a series of short robin-like phrases, such as *cherry-o-wit, cheree, sissy-a-wit, tee-oo.* Warbling vireos give a long, unbroken, drowsy warble.

Red-eyed Vireo

Warbling Vireo

fall

spring

VIREOS

YELLOW-THROATED VIREO

BLUE-HEADED VIREO

WHITE-EYED VIREO

The reclusive white-eyed vireo can often be identified by its loud, scolding song: **Spit, and see if I care. Spit.**

Yellow-throated vireos are scarce. They feed sluggishly in the upper levels of mature trees (hardwood or mixed) at forest edges and in stands of tall trees in open areas. Like other vireos, they glean insects from vegetation and take some fruit.

Yellow-throated vireos are easy to distinguish from other vireos but resemble pine warblers (p. 68). The spectacles and "swollen" bill of the vireo are good marks. The yellow eye line of the warbler extends behind the eye.

Blue-headed vireos like large areas of mature forest. Over most of their range, they live in conifers, but in the Appalachians, they also use hardwood and mixed forests. They forage sluggishly in the canopy and the underbrush.

The bold white spectacles of the **blue-headed vireo** are usually obvious. There is also a distinct contrast between the gray head and the greenish back. They are fairly numerous.

White-eyed vireos are numerous in the dense deciduous shrub associated with overgrown pastures and woodland edges. They are active and inquisitive, unlike other vireos, but often hidden in brush and brambles. The white eye of the adult can be seen at close range. A better mark for the **white-eyed vireo** is the contrasting bright yellow spectacles.

64

pine warbler p. 68

Yellow-throated
Vireo

Blue-headed Vireo

White-eyed Vireo

young

YELLOW/ WING BARS

NORTHERN PARULA

CHESTNUT-SIDED WARBLER

Every warbler has its feeding specialty and habitat preferences. Those of the northern parula (PAR-a-la) and chestnut-sided warbler are quite distinct.

The parula prefers mature forests, especially near bogs or swamps. In the South, it builds its nest in Spanish moss when available. In the North, it prefers *Usnea* lichen (old man's beard). Parulas typically feed on insects gleaned from the tips of branches in the middle or upper story of the forest. They are numerous.

The bands on the male **northern parula's** breast are easy marks. Most females and all young birds lack them but are still well marked with yellow throats, white wing bars, white eye-rings, and a triangular gold patch on the back.

The chestnut-sided warbler likes early deciduous regrowth—especially areas disturbed by farming, fire, or clear-cutting that are left to regenerate. It specializes in insects taken primarily from the underside of leaves.

The side stripes are easy marks for the **chestnut-sided warbler** when present. Only the bay-breasted warbler (p. 86) shares this feature. Old males have the longest side stripes; young females often have none. Their best marks are the distinctive lime-green upperparts, white eye-ring, and yellow wing bars.

♀ and young

Northern Parula

♂

young

Chestnut-sided Warbler

spring ♂

spring ♀

BLUE-WINGED WARBLER

PINE WARBLER

Golden-winged warblers share habitat and some range with the blue-winged. Most nest in Canada and the northern tier of states. Where range overlaps, the blue-winged is displacing the scarcer golden-winged.

The golden-winged is gray bodied, with a yellow wing patch and forehead and a dark chin and mask.

B lue-winged warblers are numerous in brushy undergrowth and small trees. They are sometimes found in deep swamps if there is sufficient undergrowth but are more common in brushy woodland edges and over-grown fields. They move slowly and can be inconspicuous gleaning insects from foliage.

The plain yellow face with a black eye line is a sure mark for the **blue-winged warbler.** In fall, the forehead is greenish, like the hind crown and back, and a faint yellow eyebrow becomes more apparent. Young birds are slightly duller than fall adults.

The pine warbler is numerous and nearly always in pines, except during migration. It creeps methodically through treetops, along branches, and on tree trunks in search of insects. It also forages on the ground.

The male **pine warbler** in spring resembles the yellow-throated vireo (p. 64), but its breast is neither as bright nor as clear, its bill is thin-ner, and the eye markings don't form specta-cles. Females and fall pine warblers are duller; young birds can lack any yellow tones. Some can resemble the fall blackpoll (p. 88) or bay-breasted warbler (p. 86) but have plain, unstreaked backs. Others have enough yellow to suggest a young myrtle warbler (p. 72).

Blue-winged Warbler

fall blackpoll
warbler p. 88

yellow-throated
vireo p. 64

Pine Warbler

spring ♂

♀

young

**BLACKBURNIAN
WARBLER**

**MAGNOLIA
WARBLER**

The blackburnian warbler and magnolia warbler are two of several closely related warblers that migrate to the cool coniferous forests of Canada and the northern US to nest. The brilliant blackburnian takes to the canopy of mature forests, while the magnolia is one of the first to colonize areas of young, second-growth conifers. Both are numerous.

Blackburnian warblers inhabit mixed forests also, and in the southern Appalachians, they accept deciduous woods. They take a variety of insects but concentrate on spruce budworms when available. The black head markings and burst of orange on the throat are eye-grabbing marks for the **blackburnian warbler.** Females are paler than males, and some young females have barely a hint of color on the throat.

In their northern range, magnolia warblers most often live in spruce forests, and like blackburnian warblers, they are common during spruce budworm outbreaks. To the south, they prefer eastern hemlocks. They are seldom more than 10 or 15 feet from the ground, feeding actively at the outer edges of a tree.

The **magnolia warbler's** wings and tail are often half-spread, displaying large white patches. Young birds have dull face and breast patterns; their yellow rump is a helpful mark.

♀

♂

Blackburnian Warbler

Magnolia Warbler

♀

young

spring ♂

**CAPE MAY
WARBLER**

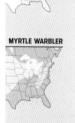

MYRTLE WARBLER

Once a species in its own right, the myrtle warbler is now lumped with the Audubon's warbler of the West as the yellow-rumped warbler.

The myrtle warbler name is still useful in differentiating the eastern birds from the yellow-chinned Audubon's form.

The Cape May and myrtle warblers are two more warblers that nest in the coniferous forest that stretches across Canada and the northern US. Over most of the US, the Cape May warbler is a scarce migrant. The myrtle warbler is abundant, with a majority of the birds overwintering in the southern US.

The Cape May warbler is a canopy specialist in tall trees. It takes many insects but is so dependent on spruce budworms that its numbers fluctuate with outbreaks.

Myrtle warblers also prefer tall trees in summer, typically in open woodlands or at forest edges. They are conifer generalists, inspecting every part of a tree for insects and flycatching as well. In winter and during migration, they accept many types of woods. Along the Atlantic coast, they are common in bayberries.

Yellow rumps are a distinguishing feature of the **Cape May** and **myrtle warblers.** The only other warbler with a yellow rump is the magnolia warbler (p. 70). Young myrtle warblers can always be separated from other warblers with yellow rumps by the patch of yellow near the shoulder. The young Cape May warbler has a paler yellow rump than the others and is the only one with fine streaks extending across the entire breast.

Cape May Warbler

♀

spring ♂

young ♀

Myrtle Warbler

♀

young

spring ♂

**YELLOW/
WING BARS**

**YELLOW-THROATED
WARBLER**

**BLACK-THROATED
GREEN WARBLER**

Yellow-throated warblers accept two very distinct habitats. Mature bottomland forests and swamps, especially those with sycamores, attract some birds. Dry upland stands of tall pines attract others. In both cases, the birds live in the upper story of tall trees. They creep along high branches, using their long bills to probe for insects in the bark. Occasionally they are seen on tree trunks.

Female and young **yellow-throated warblers** are a bit duller than the male shown but still bright and easy to identify if seen well. Birds in the Southeast have a yellow dot before the eye.

Black-throated green warblers are numerous migrants to northern conifers, and where their range extends into the southern Appalachians, they accept mixed and even pure hardwood forests. They forage primarily on small branches in the upper levels of tall trees, feeding heavily on caterpillars. A separate race, Wayne's warbler, lives in cypress swamps on the mid-Atlantic coast lowlands.

The triangular yellow face patch is the **black-throated green warbler's** most notable mark. A greenish back and crown border it. Males have an extensive black throat patch that is much reduced in females and can be absent in young birds.

Yellow-throated Warbler

Black-throated Green Warbler

♀

young

♂

**YELLOW/
FAINT BARS**

PRAIRIE WARBLER

PALM WARBLER

W ing bars are thin or can be lacking on **prairie** and **palm warblers,** but all habitually bob their tails. The behavior is very useful in identifying duller fall birds. Young prairie warblers have only vague side streaks; however, their face pattern remains distinct enough to be recognized.

In spring, palm warblers have distinctive rusty caps and broad, yellow eyebrows. The yellow form, which nests in eastern Canada and winters along the Gulf, are yellow below. On the western form, which nests in central Canada and winters from Florida to Texas and along the Atlantic, the belly is white. The bright yellow under the tail is always present and a good mark.

Palm warblers typically feed on or near the ground and use a variety of woodland, scrub, and open habitats. They usually nest in northern bogs with scattered trees and heavy undergrowth. A ground-feeding warbler that bobs its tail is almost certainly a palm warbler.

Prairie warblers like brushy undergrowth and young stands of second-growth forest. They don't inhabit western prairies but do winter in brushy areas with scattered trees. They feed on insects near the ground but not on it, in shrubs and on the lower limbs of trees.

Prairie Warbler

♀

♂

young

Palm Warbler

western form spring

fall

yellow form spring

YELLOW/ NO BARS

PROTHONOTARY WARBLER

YELLOW WARBLER

Prothonotary warblers are the only cavity-nesting warbler. When possible, they choose a cavity next to or even over water. They readily accept nest boxes.

The prothonotary warbler is seldom far from water. Golden swamp warbler is a descriptive name for this fairly numerous and lustrous bird. It also inhabits willow-lined streamsides and usually feeds on insects in the shrubs and debris near the water.

The male **prothonotary warbler's** head and breast virtually glow. His beady black eye and fairly long black bill contrast sharply. Blue-gray wings and the white under the tail are good marks separating prothonotaries from yellow warblers.

Yellow warblers are one of the most abundant and widespread warblers. They feed on insects gleaned from the young brushy growth that they inhabit. Streamside patches of willows and alders are favorite haunts, but nearly any area of scrub, shrubs, or young growth could host a yellow warbler.

Yellow warblers often give an overall yellow appearance except for the eye and the bill. The chestnut stripes on the male are not always obvious, and yellow edging on the wing feathers reduces their contrast. The distinctive yellow wing edging is a particularly good mark on individuals that aren't bright yellow — greenish yellow females and dingy young.

♀ and young

♂

Prothonotary Warbler

Yellow Warbler

♀ and young

♂

young
olive extreme

**NASHVILLE
WARBLER**

**COMMON
YELLOWTHROAT**

The mourning warbler is a scarce migrant over most of the East. It is somewhat like a Nashville warbler, but the gray extends onto the throat and breast, forming a hood.

The mourning warbler is a shy bird that feeds on or near the ground in thickets and forest edges.

The Nashville warbler visits Nashville — and most of the East — only during migration, when it is seen in open woods or brushy areas. It is fairly numerous, nesting in a variety of open woodlands, especially where underbrush is present. It will inhabit a young woodland and continue to use it until the canopy starts to close and the underbrush disappear.

A gray-headed warbler with a bright yellow throat and breast is a **Nashville warbler.** The complete white eye-ring is usually obvious; the rusty crown patch is not. Females and fall birds are slightly duller than spring males.

An abundant warbler, the common yellow-throat is wren-like — very active and often scolding while hidden in dense tangles of vegetation. The thick growth in marshes and other wet areas is a favorite habitat, and so are briar patches found in early forest regeneration.

The dramatically masked adult male **common yellowthroat** is easy to identify. Young males show a suggestion of the mask; females have none and can be hard to identify because their best mark — the pattern of yellow — is a subtle one. Yellow is limited to the throat, breast, and undertail; it does not extend onto the cheek or belly. The thin white eye-ring is another useful mark.

♀ and young

Nashville Warbler

♂

Common
Yellowthroat

young ♂

♂

♀

YELLOW/ NO BARS

CANADA WARBLER

KENTUCKY WARBLER

Few warblers actually warble. Their songs tend to be high-pitched notes and trills. A warbling song is most likely given by a vireo or finch.

Canada and Kentucky warblers both frequent the underbrush of mature forests, especially wet areas. However, Canada warblers prefer cool northern slopes and streamside shrubs, where they feed actively, often catching passing bugs flycatcher fashion. They are scarce but not particularly shy.

The Kentucky warbler is furtive, hidden in the dense underbrush of low swamps and wet ravines and bottomlands. It spends most of its time on the ground, often flicking its tail as it searches through leaf litter for insects. Kentucky warblers are fairly numerous, especially in the Mississippi Valley. Males sing energetically from a low branch.

The rich colors and bold necklace of the male **Canada warbler** make him easy to identify with a decent look. Necklaces are faint on female and young Canada warblers but always present, as are the yellow spectacles (the eye-ring is usually white). The backs of young birds can be more brownish gray than the adult's blue-gray.

Kentucky warblers are a rich yellow from chin to tail. Males have a broad black "sideburn" that is reduced in females and the young. The yellow spectacles are a good mark, and the pink legs are bright and notable.

82

♀ and young

♂

Canada Warbler

♀
and young

♂

Kentucky Warbler

WILSON'S WARBLER

HOODED WARBLER

Wilson's warblers like shrubby growth, wetlands, and an open canopy. Although they aren't always near water, especially during migration, their favorite haunts are brushy swamps, streams bordered by willows and alders, and northern bogs. Wilson's seldom feeds much above eye level, and it feeds actively, often flicking its wings like a kinglet, jerking its tail about, and flycatching.

Female **Wilson's warblers** show a trace of the male's black cap. Some don't; they and young birds are easily confused with other warblers that appear as a flash of yellow — especially female yellow and hooded warblers. The underside of Wilson's tail is yellow (the hooded's is white), and its wings are plain (the yellow warbler has yellow-edged feathers). Also note Wilson's distinct yellow eyebrow.

The hooded warbler, like Wilson's, frequents shrubby undergrowth associated with water. However, the hooded warbler prefers small openings in mature hardwood forests, especially cypress swamps in the South. It feeds actively, fanning its tail and sometimes flycatching.

Females show incomplete suggestions of the black markings on the male **hooded warbler,** but some young females are best identified by their white tail spots.

84

Wilson's Warbler

♀

♂

Hooded Warbler

♂

♀

NO YELLOW/ WING BARS

BAY-BREASTED WARBLER

CERULEAN WARBLER

Bay-breasted warblers can be ten times more common in areas of spruce budworm outbreak. Evidence indicates that the insecticide used to control the damage done by spruce budworms also damages bay-breasted warblers.

Most people in the East get to see the beautiful bay-breasted warbler only during migration. Even then, they are scarce and tend to stay in the upper level of trees. They nest in dense, preferably mature coniferous forests, where they often feed along branches near the trunk. Spruce budworms and other caterpillars are a favorite food.

Some spring female **bay-breasted warblers** have little chestnut on their sides and can be hard to identify, but the real problem is with the greenish yellow fall birds. Fall males show a faint but helpful wash of bay on the flanks; females look much like fall blackpoll warblers (p. 88) but have dark legs and feet and fainter streaks. Compare with the pine warbler (p. 68).

Cerulean warblers are scarce, scattered, and declining. They are difficult to locate even when present, since they feed primarily in the canopy of mature trees in open hardwood forests.

The stunning blue male **cerulean warbler** is unmistakable. Females have blue-gray crowns, but their backs are similar to that of the young bird shown. The young in fall are brighter green above, including the head, than the similar but larger fall bay-breasted, blackpoll (p. 88), or dull blackburnian (p. 70) warblers. Young ceruleans also have clear, unstreaked backs.

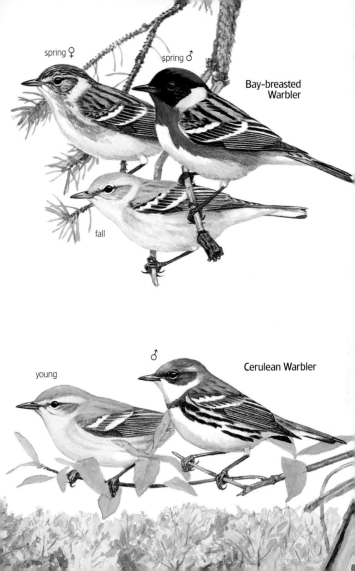

spring ♀

spring ♂

Bay-breasted
Warbler

fall

young

♂

Cerulean Warbler

NO YELLOW/ WING BARS

BLACK-AND-WHITE WARBLER

BLACKPOLL WARBLER

Black-and-white warblers are one of the earliest spring migrants, arriving while trees are still bare or budding. Blackpoll warblers are one of the latest spring migrants, waiting until trees are in full foliage.

Even if it weren't so dramatically striped, the black-and-white warbler would be notable for the way it creeps like a nuthatch along tree trunks and major branches, inspecting the bark for insects. They sometimes forage in foliage and on the ground. In summer, they are numerous in mature hardwood or mixed forests. Second growth and scrub are also used in winter and during migration.

In spring, head stripes distinguish the **black-and-white warbler** from the male blackpoll warbler. Male black-and-white warblers in spring have a black throat.

Blackpoll warblers are numerous in summer in the canopy of Canadian coniferous forests. Over nearly all the eastern US, they are migrants. In spring, they migrate in treetops. In fall, they forage at all levels and concentrate along the coast in the Northeast.

The spring female **blackpoll warbler** lacks the male's bold head pattern. The fine streaks on her back and sides are good marks, if not as dramatic as the black-and-white warbler's stripes. Note her face pattern and bright legs.

In fall, blackpoll warblers look like bay-breasted warblers (p. 86) but have pale legs and feet, darker streaking, and no buff color on the flanks. Compare with the pine warbler (p. 68).

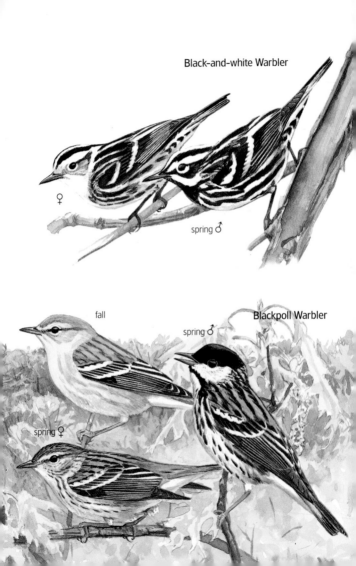

Black-and-white Warbler

♀

spring ♂

fall

Blackpoll Warbler

spring ♂

spring ♀

NO YELLOW/ NO BARS

AMERICAN REDSTART

BLACK-THROATED BLUE WARBLER

The differences between male and female black-throated blue warblers is so complete and so unusual for warblers that early ornithologists, such as Audubon, considered the sexes to be separate species.

American redstarts are numerous and found in a variety of deciduous or mixed woodlands, especially near water in deciduous second-growth woods. They forage at all levels and often flycatch, having the flat bills and bristles characteristic of flycatchers.

The orange-on-black pattern flashed by the male **American redstart** as it acrobatically forages suggests a flickering torch illuminating a black night. Or so the Spanish thought, as they named the bird *candelita*. Females are marked yellow on gray and olive upperparts. Males take two years to attain adult plumage. Yearling males resemble females but show some orange instead of yellow on the sides.

Black-throated blue warblers prefer large tracts of mature hardwood and mixed forests with heavy deciduous underbrush. Fairly numerous, they feed primarily on insects in shrubs and the lower levels of trees. They are often seen in rhododendrons in the Appalachians.

Only the small patch of white in the wings is shared by male and female **black-throated blue warblers,** and it can be lacking in young females. The long white eyebrow and partial eye-ring are the other good marks on the dull olive and buff female. Young males have a greenish tinge to their blue upperparts.

American
Redstart

Black-throated Blue
Warbler

**TENNESSEE
WARBLER**

**WORM-EATING
WARBLER**

OVENBIRD

Swainson's warbler is
scarce, secretive, and
declining in dense
southern swamps and
in Appalachian laurel
thickets. Plain-bodied
like a worm-eating
warbler, it has a rusty
cap and white
eyebrow.

Over most of the East, Tennessee warblers visit during migration. In spring, they are usually in large trees; in fall, often in shrubs. Shrubby undergrowth is also important in their choice of nesting woodlands.

Tennessee warblers are fairly numerous but declining. Plainness is one of the bird's best marks. Spring males show only a dark eye line, white eyebrow, and contrast between the gray head and olive back. Females and fall birds are duller, with some buff on the face and breast.

Worm-eating warblers prefer the shrubby undergrowth of mature hardwood or mixed forests on hillsides and ravines. They seach dead leaves for insects and sometimes creep over tree trunks and limbs. Their name refers to caterpillars, not earthworms. The boldly striped head and plain body are easy marks for the scarce **worm-eating warbler.**

Ovenbirds are primarily ground feeders that pump their tails as they walk. They are numerous in large mature forests with sparse underbrush. Most like dry hardwood forest, but they occur in wet areas and, in the North, conifers.

The heavy black streaking on the white underparts, the distinctive orange crown bordered in black, and the white eye-ring are all good marks for the **ovenbird.**

young in fall

Tennessee Warbler

spring ♂

Worm-eating
Warbler

Ovenbird

**NO YELLOW/
NO BARS**

**NORTHERN
WATERTHRUSH**

**LOUISIANA
WATERTHRUSH**

The Louisiana
waterthrush tends to
have a cleaner throat
than the northern.
Breast streaks on the
northern continue
onto the throat.

Waterthrushes are warblers, not thrushes, although they feed primarily on the ground and prefer wet forested habitats, as thrushes often do. Thrushes (pp. 56–59) are spotted below; waterthrushes are streaked. And waterthrushes continually bob their bodies and wag their tails as they walk.

The northern waterthrush is numerous in cool northern bogs, swamps, and wooded wetlands. It likes heavy ground cover. During migration, it might be found wherever there is water and cover. The Louisiana waterthrush prefers running streams in hilly hardwood forests but is also found in cypress swamps and wooded bottomlands near the sort of still water that the northern waterthrush prefers. Both birds often feed while wading, scouring the banks and floating debris for insects. Where ranges overlap, they can be found in the same area.

The waterthrushes can be reliably separated by plumage. Any that are yellowish below are northerns. The best marks for birds that are clear white are the flank color (buff in the Louisiana) and the eyebrow. As it extends behind the eye on the **Louisiana waterthrush,** the eyebrow widens. On the **northern waterthrush,** it becomes narrower. Breast streaking is a little bolder on northern waterthrushes, and the legs are darker, not pinkish.

Northern
Waterthrush

Louisiana Waterthrush

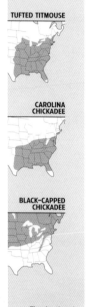

TUFTED TITMOUSE

CAROLINA CHICKADEE

BLACK-CAPPED CHICKADEE

The rise that the artist, Larry McQueen, shows on the hind neck of the black-capped is a typical chickadee behavior.

Titmice and chickadees are closely related and behave much alike. They occupy a variety of deciduous and mixed woodlands, from scattered trees to interior forest. In summer, they feed heavily on insects gleaned from twigs, limbs, and tree trunks. The tufted titmouse also forages on the ground.

In fall, when bugs and larvae become hard to find and the year's crop of seeds and nuts ripens, titmice and chickadees adapt to the new bounty. Many visit backyards to feed on sunflower seeds set out for them. They often carefully store seeds under loose bark or in crevices along a limb. Tests on black-capped chickadees show that they remember caches for up to a month.

The perky crest and coal black eye of the **tufted titmouse** are sufficient marks for this bold little bird in the East.

There is only a narrow band where black-capped and Carolina chickadee ranges overlap. However, the two birds can be separated by plumage as well as geography. Check the wings. The **Carolina chickadee** shows only a minor amount of white or pale streaking on the folded wing, but the **black-capped chickadee** has distinct white in the folded wing and often forming a bar on the shoulder.

Tufted Titmouse

Carolina Chickadee

Black-capped
Chickadee

RUBY-CROWNED KINGLET

GOLDEN-CROWNED KINGLET

BLUE-GRAY GNATCATCHER

In the East and Midwest, golden-crowned kinglets have increased their nesting range to the south in extensive plantings of spruce.

The tiny kinglets and gnatcatchers are closely related in spite of their different shapes. Kinglets nest in northern conifers and are numerous in a wide variety of woodlands in winter and during migration. They feed from shrubs to treetops. The ruby-crowned kinglet takes a few seeds in winter, but all kinglets manage to find hidden larvae and insect matter even in cold and snowy weather.

The color of its crown and the white eyebrow are good marks for the **golden-crowned kinglet. Ruby-crowned kinglets** are more nondescript; only the male shows red, and it is usually concealed. The tiny bill, plump body, short tail, and wing-flicking habit give the ruby-crowned a different look from the warblers with which it might be confused. The clinching marks are a white eye-ring broken at the top and a white wing bar bordered below by a dark patch — the kinglet patch.

The **blue-gray gnatcatcher** is long, slender, and very active. It is more tail than bird. The white underside flashes as the tail is twitched and cocked expressively. Both sexes have a white eye-ring; males have a narrow black eyebrow and a blue-gray crown. Gnatcatchers pick bugs from leaves and snatch some in flight. They are fairly numerous in deciduous trees and shrubs, especially near water.

Ruby-crowned Kinglet

Golden-crowned Kinglet

Blue-gray Gnatcatcher

summer ♂

CARDINAL & TOWHEE

CARDINAL

EASTERN TOWHEE

The eastern towhee has declined at a faster rate than any other bird in the East. Even though the northeastern population has declined approximately 85 percent in the last 30 years, the birds remain relatively numerous.

Cardinals are residents in the shrubby growth at woodland edges and along streams, as well as in parks, roadsides, and suburban backyards. Seeds and insects are taken from the ground and bushes. The cardinal's range has expanded northward because of the availability of sunflower seeds at feeders, allowing them to overwinter.

Even the brownish female **cardinal** is easily recognized by her crest, the red in her wings and tail, and her heavy conical bill. Young birds look like females but have dull bills instead of the bright orange-red bills of females.

Eastern towhees feed in leaf litter and are almost always hidden in shadows and shrubs. The shrubs can be in the open, at a woodland edge, or part of a forest understory. Drier areas are preferred, but towhees can be found at swamp edges as well. Seeds, bugs, and fruits are all consumed.

The rusty-colored sides are good marks for adult **eastern towhees.** Males have black hoods and backs; females, brown. Long black tails with white in the corners are prominent marks for both the adults and the streaked, brown young birds. Their song, a distinctive *drink-your-tea,* or their namesake *tow-hee* call is often the best clue to the bird's presence.

100

♀

♂

Cardinal

Eastern Towhee

♀

♂

young

GROSBEAKS

ROSE-BREASTED
GROSBEAK

BLUE GROSBEAK

Evening grosbeaks can be fairly numerous nesters in mixed and coniferous woods from the Canadian border states northward. In winter, some often come south, especially to sunflower seed feeders.

Male evening grosbeaks are dark brown and yellow with white wing patches. Females are grayer.

Big finches with very heavy bills, the grosbeaks on this page are summer visitors from the tropics. Rose-breasted grosbeaks like woodland edges where shrubs and undergrowth meet good-sized trees. Streamsides are especially favored. They eat insects as much as seeds, gathering them from all levels.

In spring, adult male **rose-breasted grosbeaks** are impressively beautiful and easy to identify. In fall, they look more like females but keep their black wings and tail and a rose blush on their breasts. The female has striped underparts, like many smaller finches. The large bill and distinct head stripes are her best marks. Young birds in fall resemble the female; young males have buff breasts. Males of all ages have red underwings; females, yellow.

Blue grosbeaks are scarce. They occupy various woodland edge habitats and are fond of thick, low vegetation. They also gather in weedy, overgrown fields and agricultural lands. Insects are eaten, as well as seeds.

Male **blue grosbeaks,** which often sing from an exposed perch, can look black in bad light. Females are largely brown but have some blue on their wings, tail, and rump. Their size, heavy bill, and rusty brown wing bars distinguish them in all plumages.

Rose-breasted Grosbeak

young ♂ in first fall

♀

♂

♀ ♂

Blue Grosbeak

yearling ♂
in spring

♂

♀

BUNTINGS

PAINTED BUNTING

INDIGO BUNTING

Buntings are fairly numerous birds of dense shrubs and weeds, including those found streamside and at woodland edges. The painted bunting likes wetlands but also lives in dry areas and is a regular in southern gardens. It is a shy bird and often hidden. Weed seeds are a principal food, and it gleans insects from low vegetation as well.

Seen in the shadows, the adult male **painted bunting's** brilliant colors can be very muted. Females are our only sparrow-like birds with green upperparts. Males take two years to acquire their brilliant dress. As yearlings, they look like females but can attract mates by singing and breed. Females don't sing.

Indigo buntings forage from the ground up. Like painted buntings, they take weed seeds, but they feed more heavily on insects in summer and will go to the treetops to get them. Males often sing from a prominent perch.

In good light, spring male **indigo buntings** are shiny blue; in bad light, they look black. Females are best identified by their lack of distinguishing marks. They are an evenly warm brown, sparrow-like bird with only vague streaking below and hints of blue in the wings and tail. Young males and fall adult males are brown with varying amounts of blue.

young

Painted Bunting

♂

♀

Indigo Bunting

yearling ♂
in spring

fall ♂

spring ♂

♀

PINE SISKIN

AMERICAN GOLDFINCH

Over most of the East, the pine siskin is an irregular winter visitor from northern conifers, where they are numerous. Although flocks reach the Gulf Coast, they do so only rarely. After some winter invasions, birds remain to nest before returning north.

During their winter wanderings, flocks of siskins can be found in a variety of habitats — thickets, woods, residential areas — but they prefer conifers. Insects and small seeds are taken from ground level to the treetops.

The yellow on the **pine siskin** is mostly hidden in the folded wing. In flight, the bright flashes of yellow are a sure mark for these extensively streaked birds. Like goldfinches, they bounce along in undulating flight.

American goldfinches in summer are easily recognized by the brilliant males, the only yellow birds with black wings. Females are much duller and lack the black forehead. In winter, both male and female have brownish bodies with only hints of yellow.

Goldfinches are abundant in weedy fields and floodplains, where they feed heavily on the seeds of thistles and dandelions. They often use mature, scattered trees and forest edges for shelter.

Pine Siskin

American Goldfinch

summer ♀

summer ♂

winter ♂

CROSSBILLS

WHITE-WINGED CROSSBILL

RED CROSSBILL

The different forms of red crossbills—five different ones have been recognized in the East—might be separate species. Ornithologists have discovered that different forms have subtly different call notes, which may help keep them from interbreeding.

The unusual bills of the white-winged and red crossbills are specialized for extracting seeds from conifer cones. The cone is typically held in one foot as the bird spreads each scale open, exposing the seed at the base to a swipe of the bird's tongue.

Crossbills wander in flocks, ever searching for a ripe crop of conifer cones. Where food abounds they nest. In winter, they occasionally invade areas far south of their normal range, presumably in search of food. Flocks of either species are likely in the East.

The cones of different conifers vary, and so do the curved mandibles of the crossbills that feed on them. White-winged crossbills are spruce and tamarack specialists. Flocks of red crossbills have different preferences among pines, spruces, and hemlocks; bill shape (and overall size) varies accordingly.

Adult male **white-winged crossbills** have a rose-red body. The broad white wing bars are easy marks separating the dull females and young birds from female red crossbills. The upper wing bar is sometimes hidden. Most male **red crossbills** have brick-red bodies, but some are reddish yellow and even greenish. Females are grayish olive with greenish or greenish yellow tints on the breast and rump.

108

White-winged Crossbill

young ♂

♂

♀

Red Crossbill

♂

young

♀

RED FINCHES

COMMON REDPOLL

HOUSE FINCH

PURPLE FINCH

House finches are a western species introduced on Long Island, New York, in the 1940s. They have proliferated in the East, partly at the expense of the purple finch.

Over most of the East, the **common redpoll** is an irregular winter visitor recognized by its red cap. Invading flocks search for weed seeds and often use trees (especially streamside birches) and shrubs for cover.

House finches are abundant but are rarely far from suburban or rural areas. Purple finches also live on developed land but are widespread in open woodlands as well. They are only fairly numerous and declining in the East. The females are plain, brown-striped birds that require even more care in identification.

The best mark for the male **house finch** is the distinct brown streaking on its sides and belly. **Purple finches** have blurry, reddish side streaks at most. The shade of red on the male house finch varies. It often tends toward orange and can rarely be yellow. The color on the head is concentrated in a U-shaped band on the forehead and eyebrows. On the purple finch, the red extends onto the crown, nape, and back and tends to be more wine-colored.

The contrast of the broad white eyebrow and whisker stripe on the female purple finch is her best mark. The face of the female house finch is much plainer; her breast streaks are a bit finer and extend all the way under her less deeply notched tail.

Common Redpoll

♀

♂

House Finch

♀

♂

Purple Finch

♂

♀

JUNCO & SPARROW

SLATE-COLORED JUNCO

FOX SPARROW

Western forms of the dark-eyed junco and fox sparrow have different plumage colors than the eastern forms.

The form of the dark-eyed junco seen in the East is known as the slate-colored junco. Many people call them snowbirds — with the first snows, they appear in large numbers over a broad area of the East and remain until spring.

In the Appalachians, juncos live year-round in rhododendron thickets. They feed primarily on the ground, taking small seeds and, in summer, many bugs as well. On their nesting grounds, they live in open woodlands and forest edges.

The white outer tail feathers and belly are easy marks for **slate-colored juncos.** Males are, indeed, slate-colored; females are browner and often show some contrast between the sides, back, and hood.

Fox sparrows are also ground feeders, but solitary and much more furtive than juncos. They are fairly numerous in the underbrush of overgrown fields, woodland edges, and streamsides, foraging in the leaf litter.

The breast streaking and central spot make the **fox sparrow** look like a large version of the song sparrow (p. 118). They are a very reddish brown in the East, and the blunt-tipped, red-brown tail is a good mark.

Slate-colored Junco

♂

♀

Fox Sparrow

SPARROWS

WHITE-THROATED SPARROW

WHITE-CROWNED SPARROW

The lark sparrow is scarce in the East. It is primarily a scrubland species but also occupies open woodlands.

Lark sparrows have black-and-white striped heads that include chestnut patches. Their breasts are clear except for a single central dot.

Prominent black and white crown stripes distinguish adult white-throated and white-crowned sparrows. White-throated sparrows are much more common in most areas of the East but a bit more secretive than white-crowns.

Both white-crowned and white-throated sparrows are winter visitors in much of the East. They are never far from thick cover and feed primarily on the ground. In summer, the white-thoated likes openings in coniferous and mixed forests with dense vegetation.

White-throated and white-crowned sparrows are both a little larger than most sparrows. In addition to the crown stripes, the **white-throated sparrow** has a white throat, and most have a spot of yellow in front of the eye. The **white-crowned sparrow** lacks the white throat but has a prominent dull pinkish bill. ("Gambel's" is a western form that has white in front of the eye, not black as in eastern birds.)

Heads of both species can be striped in shades of brown instead of black and white. Brown stripes on a white-crowned sparrow are the mark of a young bird. On a white-throated, brown stripes are also worn by many adults. Interestingly, white-throats mate with individuals having the opposite color crown stripes.

very young
late summer

White-throated Sparrow

tan-striped
form

very young
late summer

White-crowned Sparrow

young

Gambel's
form

SPARROWS

TREE SPARROW

FIELD SPARROW

CHIPPING SPARROW

The tree sparrow suffers from an inappropriate name. It feeds on or near the ground, like its relatives, and is more associated with weed seeds and brush than with trees.

Not all plumages of these closely related, small, slim sparrows show a rusty cap or crown stripes, but most do. All three have fairly long, notched tails (tail shape is a good clue for identifying small brown sparrows), and all flock in winter. They feed on or near the ground, primarily on weed seeds.

The **tree sparrow** has a prominent "stickpin" on its plain breast. It is a numerous winter visitor to fields, suburbs, and open woodlands.

Best marks for the **field sparrow** are its bright pink bill and the white eye-ring. The eye-ring on the relatively plain face gives the bird a blank look. They are shier and less numerous than tree and chipping sparrows. Field sparrows do inhabit fields but also occupy forest clearings and edges.

Chipping sparrows have a bright rusty crown in summer, bordered by a white eyebrow and a black eye line that extends all the way to the bill. The face and crown are duller in winter, especially in first-winter birds. The black eye line is not as bold in winter but still extends in front of the eye.

Chipping sparrows like grassy clearings and edges bordered by shrubs and forest. They are numerous in conifer scrub and visit short grass and bare areas in some suburbs.

Tree Sparrow

very young
late summer

Field Sparrow

very young
late summer

Chipping Sparrow

very young
late summer

1st winter

SPARROWS

SONG SPARROW

SWAMP SPARROW

Lincoln's sparrow is a close relative of the song sparrow and a scarce eastern wetland sparrow. It has finer breast and whisker streaks than the song sparrow, a pale buff wash on the breast and cheek, and a small breast spot at best.

Song and swamp sparrows are closely related. Both have long, rounded tails that they pump in flight, and both are usually solitary. The **song sparrow** is noted for the central spot on its streaked breast, but it shares that feature with the fox sparrow (p. 112). Note the heavy, dark whisker stripe.

The **swamp sparrow** has a rusty tail and wings in all plumages. In spring, it has a bright rusty cap and broad gray eyebrow. Dull rusty crown stripes remain on adults in winter. The contrast between the gray breast, white throat, and brown sides makes each of these features seem more prominent.

Swamps sparrows are well named; they are seldom far from shallow standing water. Cattail marshes, northern bogs, and brackish coastal marshes are some of the preferred wetlands. They often feed and live in dense grasses and reeds at the water's edge, taking insects and seeds as available. In winter, they sometimes feed in fields of dry scrub.

Song sparrows prefer wetlands also, but aren't as closely tied to the water's edge as the swamp sparrow. They like the brush and scrub that surround and adjoin wet and moist areas. Song sparrows are more numerous and not as secretive as swamp sparrows.

Song Sparrow

very young
late summer

Swamp Sparrow

young

winter

summer

CHECK-LIST AND INDEX

How many species of birds have you identified? Keeping a record is the only way to know. Sooner or later, even the most casual bird-watcher makes notes of the species seen on a trip or in a day. People keep backyard lists, year lists, state and provincial lists, every kind of checklist. All serious birders maintain a life list. Seeing your life list grow can become part of the pleasure of bird-watching. The pages that follow are designed to serve as your checklist of eastern trailside songbirds as well as an index to their illustrations in this guide.

English names used in this guide and listed in the index are the familiar names used in common conversation. For the most part, they are the same as the formal English names adopted by the American Ornithologists' Union in the seventh edition of their *Check-list of North American Birds,* 1998.

When the formal AOU English name differs from the common name used in this guide, the AOU English name is given on the second line of the index entry. The Latin names in italics are the AOU's scientific names.

✓ Species	Date	Location

○ **R**ED-WINGED **B**LACKBIRD 50
Agelaius phoeniceus

○ **R**USTY **B**LACKBIRD 48
Euphagus carolinus

○ **E**ASTERN **B**LUEBIRD 60
Sialia sialis

○ **I**NDIGO **B**UNTING 104
Passerina cyanea

○ **P**AINTED **B**UNTING 104
Passerina ciris

○ **C**ARDINAL 100
Northern Cardinal
Cardinalis cardinalis

○ **C**ATBIRD 60
Gray Catbird
Dumetella carolinensis

○ **C**HAT 60
Yellow-breasted Chat
Icteria virens

○ **B**LACK-CAPPED **C**HICKADEE 96
Poecile atricapillus

○ **C**AROLINA **C**HICKADEE 96
Poecile carolinensis

○ **B**ROWN-HEADED **C**OWBIRD 48
Molothrus ater

○ **B**ROWN **C**REEPER 32
Certhia americana

○ **R**ED **C**ROSSBILL 108
Loxia curvirostra

○ **W**HITE-WINGED **C**ROSSBILL 108
Loxia leucoptera

○ **A**MERICAN **C**ROW 44
Corvus brachyrhynchos

○ **Y**ELLOW-BILLED **C**UCKOO 40
Coccyzus americanus

✓ Species		Date	Location
○ HOUSE FINCH *Carpodacus mexicanus*	110		
○ PURPLE FINCH *Carpodacus purpureus*	110		
○ YELLOW-SHAFTED FLICKER Northern Flicker *Colaptes auratus*	30		
○ EMPIDONAX FLYCATCHERS genus *Empidonax*	38		
○ GREAT CRESTED FLYCATCHER *Myiarchus crinitus*	36		
○ OLIVE-SIDED FLYCATCHER *Contopus cooperi*	36		
○ BLUE-GRAY GNATCATCHER *Polioptila caerulea*	98		
○ AMERICAN GOLDFINCH *Carduelis tristis*	106		
○ COMMON GRACKLE *Quiscalus quiscula*	48		
○ BLUE GROSBEAK *Guiraca caerulea*	102		
○ ROSE-BREASTED GROSBEAK *Pheucticus ludovicianus*	102		
○ RUBY-THROATED HUMMINGBIRD *Archilochus colubris*	22		
○ BLUE JAY *Cyanocitta cristata*	46		
○ SLATE-COLORED JUNCO Dark-eyed Junco *Junco hyemalis*	112		
○ EASTERN KINGBIRD *Tyrannus tyrannus*	36		
○ GOLDEN-CROWNED KINGLET *Regulus satrapa*	98		

✓ Species	Date	Location

○ **R**UBY-CROWNED **K**INGLET 98
  Regulus calendula

○ **M**OCKINGBIRD 46
  Mimus polyglottos

○ **R**ED-BREASTED **N**UTHATCH 32
  Sitta canadensis

○ **W**HITE-BREASTED **N**UTHATCH 32
  Sitta carolinensis

○ **B**ALTIMORE **O**RIOLE 52
  Icterus galbula

○ **O**RCHARD **O**RIOLE 52
  Icterus spurius

○ **O**VENBIRD 92
  Seiurus aurocapillus

○ **N**ORTHERN **P**ARULA 66
  Parula americana

○ **E**ASTERN **P**HOEBE 38
  Sayornis phoebe

○ **C**OMMON **R**EDPOLL 110
  Carduelis flammea

○ **A**MERICAN **R**EDSTART 90
  Setophaga ruticilla

○ **R**OBIN 56
  American Robin
  Turdus migratorius

○ **Y**ELLOW-BELLIED **S**APSUCKER 30
  Sphyrapicus varius

○ **L**OGGERHEAD **S**HRIKE 34
  Lanius ludovicianus

○ **P**INE **S**ISKIN 106
  Carduelis pinus

○ **C**HIPPING **S**PARROW 116
  Spizella passerina

○ **F**IELD **S**PARROW 116
  Spizella pusilla

✓ Species		Date	Location
○ Fox **S**parrow *Passerella iliaca*	112	....	....
○ Song **S**parrow *Melospiza melodia*	118	....	....
○ Swamp **S**parrow *Melospiza georgiana*	118	....	....
○ Tree **S**parrow American Tree Sparrow *Spizella arborea*	116	....	....
○ White-crowned **S**parrow *Zonotrichia leucophrys*	114	....	....
○ White-throated **S**parrow *Zonotrichia albicollis*	114	....	....
○ **S**tarling European Starling *Sturnus vulgaris*	50	....	....
○ Rough-winged **S**wallow Northern Rough-winged Swallow *Stelgidopteryx serripennis*	22	....	....
○ Tree **S**wallow *Tachycineta bicolor*	22	....	....
○ Chimney **S**wift *Chaetura pelagica*	22	....	....
○ Scarlet **T**anager *Piranga olivacea*	54	....	....
○ Summer **T**anager *Piranga rubra*	54	....	....
○ Brown **T**hrasher *Toxostoma rufum*	40	....	....
○ Hermit **T**hrush *Catharus guttatus*	58	....	....
○ Swainson's **T**hrush *Catharus ustulatus*	58	....	....
○ Wood **T**hrush *Hylocichla mustelina*	56	....	....

✓ Species	Date	Location

○ **TUFTED TITMOUSE** 96
  Baeolophus bicolor

○ **EASTERN TOWHEE** 100
  Pipilo erythrophthalmus

○ **VEERY** 58
  Catharus fuscescens

○ **BLUE-HEADED VIREO** 64
  Vireo solitarius

○ **RED-EYED VIREO** 62
  Vireo olivaceus

○ **WARBLING VIREO** 62
  Vireo gilvus

○ **WHITE-EYED VIREO** 64
  Vireo griseus

○ **YELLOW-THROATED VIREO** 64
  Vireo flavifrons

○ **BAY-BREASTED WARBLER** 86
  Dendroica castanea

○ **CERULEAN WARBLER** 86
  Dendroica cerulea

○ **BLACK-AND-WHITE WARBLER** 88
  Mniotilta varia

○ **BLACKBURNIAN WARBLER** 70
  Dendroica fusca

○ **BLACKPOLL WARBLER** 88
  Dendroica striata

○ **BLACK-THROATED BLUE WARBLER** 90
  Dendroica caerulescens

○ **BLACK-THROATED GREEN WARBLER** 74
  Dendroica virens

○ **BLUE-WINGED WARBLER** 68
  Vermivora pinus

○ **CANADA WARBLER** 82
  Wilsonia canadensis

✓ Species		Date	Location
○ CAPE MAY WARBLER *Dendroica tigrina*	72	....	
○ CHESTNUT–SIDED WARBLER *Dendroica pensylvanica*	66	....	
○ HOODED WARBLER *Wilsonia citrina*	84	....	
○ KENTUCKY WARBLER *Oporornis formosus*	82	....	
○ MAGNOLIA WARBLER *Dendroica magnolia*	70	....	
○ MYRTLE WARBLER Yellow-rumped Warbler *Dendroica coronata*	72	....	
○ NASHVILLE WARBLER *Vermivora ruficapilla*	80	....	
○ PALM WARBLER *Dendroica palmarum*	76	....	
○ PINE WARBLER *Dendroica pinus*	68	....	
○ PRAIRIE WARBLER *Dendroica discolor*	76	....	
○ PROTHONOTARY WARBLER *Protonotaria citrea*	78	....	
○ TENNESSEE WARBLER *Vermivora peregrina*	92	....	
○ WILSON'S WARBLER *Wilsonia pusilla*	84	....	
○ WORM–EATING WARBLER *Helmitheros vermivorus*	92	....	
○ YELLOW WARBLER *Dendroica petechia*	78	....	
○ YELLOW–THROATED WARBLER *Dendroica dominica*	74	....	
○ LOUISIANA WATERTHRUSH *Seiurus motacilla*	94	....	....

✓ Species	Date	Location
○ NORTHERN WATERTHRUSH 94 *Seiurus noveboracensis*	....	....
○ CEDAR WAXWING 34 *Bombycilla cedrorum*	....	....
○ DOWNY WOODPECKER 26 *Picoides pubescens*	....	....
○ HAIRY WOODPECKER 26 *Picoides villosus*	....	....
○ PILEATED WOODPECKER 24 *Dryocopus pileatus*	....	....
○ RED-BELLIED WOODPECKER 28 *Melanerpes carolinus*	....	....
○ RED-HEADED WOODPECKER 28 *Melanerpes erythrocephalus*	....	....
○ EASTERN WOOD-PEWEE 38 *Contopus virens*	....	....
○ CAROLINA WREN 42 *Thryothorus ludovicianus*	....	....
○ HOUSE WREN 42 *Troglodytes aedon*	....	....
○ WINTER WREN 42 *Troglodytes troglodytes*	....	....
○ COMMON YELLOWTHROAT 80 *Geothlypis trichas*	....	....

Want to Help Conserve Birds?

It's as Easy as ABC!

By becoming a member of the American Bird Conservancy, you can help ensure work is being done to protect many of the species in this field guide. You can receive *Bird Conservation* magazine quarterly to learn about bird conservation throughout the Americas and *World Birdwatch* magazine for information on international bird conservation.

Make a difference to birds.
Copy this card and mail to the address listed below.

☐ **Yes,** I want to become a member and receive *Bird Conservation* magazine.
A check in the amount of $18 is enclosed.

☐ **Yes,** I want to become an International member of ABC and receive both *Bird Conservation* and *World Birdwatch* magazines.
A check in the amount of $40 is enclosed.

NAME

ADDRESS

CITY/STATE/ZIP CODE

Return to: American Bird Conservancy
1250 24th Street NW, Suite 400; Washington, DC 20037
or call **1-888-BIRD-MAG** or e-mail: abc@abcbirds.org

Memberships are tax deductible to the extent allowable by law.